A COMPREHENSIVE GUIDE TO UNDERSTANDING CYBERSECURITY

Protecting Yourself In The Digital World

D. L. Freeman

Cover image by: Cliff Hang

INTRODUCTION

In this comprehensive book, we will explore the fundamentals of cybersecurity, the risks posed by cybercriminals, and the best practices to protect yourself from becoming a victim of cybercrime. From understanding the current state of cyber threats to implementing robust security measures, this guide aims to equip you with the knowledge and tools necessary to safeguard your digital life.

Whether you are a beginner looking to enhance your cybersecurity knowledge or an experienced user seeking a refresher, this book will cover essential topics such as password security, two-factor authentication (2FA), phishing email security, secure web browsing, mobile device security, and more. We will also delve into emerging cybersecurity trends and technologies shaping the digital landscape.

By the end of this book, you will have a solid foundation in cybersecurity practices, empowering you to navigate the digital world with confidence and protect your personal information from cyber threats. Remember, being proactive in cybersecurity is the key to staying safe online. Let us embark on this journey together and fortify your digital defenses!

CONTENTS

CHAPTER 1: INTRODUCTION TO CYBERSECURITY

What is Cybersecurity?

In today's interconnected world, where technology plays a vital role in our personal and professional lives, cybersecurity has become a crucial aspect of maintaining a safe digital environment. Cybersecurity refers to the practice of protecting computers, servers, mobile devices, networks, and data from unauthorized access, damage, or theft. It encompasses a wide range of measures and techniques designed to safeguard the confidentiality, integrity, and availability of information.

Why is Cybersecurity Important?

The increasing reliance on technology and the pervasive nature of the internet have brought about numerous benefits, but they have also exposed individuals, organizations, and governments to various cyber threats. Cyberattacks have the potential to cause significant financial losses, reputational damage, and even disrupt critical infrastructure.

Here are Some Reasons Why Cybersecurity is Essential:

Protecting Confidential Information: Cybersecurity ensures that sensitive information, such as personal data, financial details, and intellectual property, remains secure and out of the hands of malicious actors.

Preserving Privacy: In an era of pervasive surveillance and data collection, cybersecurity safeguards personal privacy by preventing unauthorized access to private communications and online activities.

Safeguarding Financial Assets: Cybercriminals target financial institutions, businesses, and individuals to gain unauthorized access to financial accounts, steal funds, or engage in fraudulent activities. Effective cybersecurity measures help prevent such attacks.

Maintaining Business Continuity: Organizations heavily rely on digital systems and data for their day-to-day operations. A cybersecurity breach can disrupt business processes, leading to financial losses and reputational damage.

Protecting National Security: Cybersecurity is crucial for governments and critical infrastructure sectors to defend against cyber threats that may pose risks to national security, public safety, and economic stability.

Preventing Identity Theft: Cybercriminals often target personal information to conduct identity theft, which can lead to financial ruin and significant personal distress. Robust cybersecurity measures help mitigate this risk.

Promoting Trust and Confidence: Cybersecurity practices inspire trust and confidence among individuals, businesses, and governments, fostering a secure digital environment for communication, commerce, and collaboration.

In summary, cybersecurity is vital because it helps protect sensitive information, preserves privacy, safeguards financial assets, ensures business continuity, protects national security, prevents identity theft, and promotes trust and confidence in the digital realm. By implementing effective cybersecurity measures, individuals and organizations can mitigate the risks posed by cyber threats and navigate the digital landscape securely.

The Current State of Cybercriminals

The landscape of cybercriminals is ever evolving, with malicious actors constantly adapting their tactics to exploit vulnerabilities and gain unauthorized access to valuable information. Understanding the targets and tactics employed by cybercriminals is crucial for implementing effective cybersecurity measures.

Targets of Cybercriminals

Individuals: Cybercriminals target individuals to steal personal information, including financial data, login credentials, and Social Security numbers. They may also engage in identity theft, online harassment, and extortion. Individuals who are not adequately protected become easy targets for phishing attacks, malware infections, and social engineering scams.

Small and Medium-sized Enterprises (SMEs): SMEs often have limited resources dedicated to cybersecurity, making them attractive targets for cybercriminals. Attackers may exploit vulnerabilities in their systems to gain unauthorized access, steal sensitive data, or launch ransomware attacks. SMEs may also serve as entry points to larger organizations through supply chain attacks.

Large Enterprises and Corporations: Cybercriminals frequently target large enterprises and corporations due to the potential for significant financial gains and the wealth of valuable data they possess. Breaches in large organizations can result in severe financial losses, reputational damage, and legal consequences. Cybercriminals may employ advanced techniques and persistent attacks to breach the defenses of these targets.

Government and Critical Infrastructure: Nation-state actors and organized cybercriminal groups target government agencies and critical infrastructure sectors, including energy, healthcare, transportation, and finance. Their objectives may range from espionage and stealing classified information to disrupting essential services and causing chaos.

Tactics Employed by Cybercriminals

Phishing Attacks: Phishing is a prevalent tactic where cybercriminals send deceptive emails or messages pretending to be from trusted sources, aiming to trick individuals into revealing sensitive information, such as passwords, credit card details, or login credentials.

Malware Attacks: Malware, including viruses, worms, Trojans, and ransomware, is used to gain unauthorized access, compromise systems, and steal data. Cybercriminals distribute malware through infected email attachments, malicious websites, or software vulnerabilities.

Social Engineering: Social engineering techniques manipulate human psychology to trick individuals into divulging sensitive information or granting unauthorized access. This includes tactics like pretexting, baiting, and tailgating.

Insider Threats: Insiders with authorized access to systems and data may pose a significant threat. They can intentionally or unintentionally compromise security by leaking sensitive information, misusing privileges, or falling victim to social engineering.

Distributed Denial-of-Service (DDoS) Attacks: DDoS attacks overwhelm target systems or networks with a flood of traffic, rendering them inaccessible to legitimate users. These attacks can disrupt online services, cause financial losses, or function as a smokescreen for other cybercriminal activities.

Advanced Persistent Threats (APTs): APTs are long-term targeted attacks conducted by skilled adversaries, often with nation-state backing. They involve a combination of sophisticated techniques, including zero-day exploits, custom malware, and persistent surveillance, to gain unauthorized access to sensitive information.

Exploiting Software Vulnerabilities: Cybercriminals exploit vulnerabilities in software, operating systems, or applications to gain unauthorized access or execute malicious code. They may target unpatched systems or zero-day vulnerabilities for which no security patches are available.

It is crucial to stay informed about the evolving tactics and targets of cybercriminals. By understanding their methods, individuals and organizations can implement appropriate cybersecurity measures to protect themselves against potential threats.

Actual Examples of Cyber Exploits

SolarWinds Supply Chain Attack (December 2020): In late 2020, it was discovered that cybercriminals had compromised the software supply chain of SolarWinds, a leading IT management software provider. The attackers injected malicious code into SolarWinds' software updates, which were then distributed to numerous organizations, including government agencies and Fortune 500 companies. This breach allowed the attackers to gain unauthorized access to sensitive data and conduct espionage activities.

Colonial Pipeline Ransomware Attack (May 2021): In May 2021, Colonial Pipeline, one of the largest fuel pipeline operators in the United States, fell victim to a ransomware attack. The cybercriminal group known as DarkSide infiltrated Colonial Pipeline's network, encrypting critical systems, and demanding a ransom payment in exchange for the decryption key. The attack disrupted fuel supplies along the East Coast of the United States and highlighted the vulnerability of critical infrastructure to cyber threats.

Dish Network Ransomware Attack (February 2023): Dish Network confirmed that it had been the victim of a ransomware attack. The attack affected Dish's internal systems, as well as its websites and customer service systems. As a result of the attack, Dish customers were unable to access their accounts or make payments. Dish has not released any information about the specific ransomware strain that was used in the attack. However, the company has said that it is working with law enforcement to investigate the incident.

T-Mobile Data Breach (March 2023): T-Mobile announced that it had experienced a data breach that exposed the personal information of over 40 million customers. The breach was caused by a misconfiguration in T-Mobile's cloud infrastructure, which allowed an unauthorized third party to access customer data, including names, addresses, Social Security numbers, and driver's license numbers. T-Mobile has taken steps to secure its systems and is working with law enforcement to investigate the incident. The company has also offered free credit monitoring and identity theft protection to affected customers.

CHAPTER 2: COMMON CYBERSECURITY RISKS

I n the digital landscape, various cybersecurity risks pose significant threats to individuals and organizations. Understanding these risks is essential for implementing effective security measures. Here are some common cybersecurity risks:

Malware Attacks:

Malware refers to malicious software designed to disrupt, damage, or gain unauthorized access to computer systems and networks. Common types of malware include viruses, worms, Trojans, and ransomware. Malware can be distributed through email attachments, infected websites, or compromised software. Once infected, malware can compromise data integrity, steal sensitive information, or render systems inoperable.

Phishing Attacks:

Phishing attacks involve cybercriminals posing as trustworthy entities to trick individuals into revealing sensitive information such as passwords, credit card details, or social security numbers. These attacks are typically conducted through deceptive emails, text messages, or fraudulent websites. Phishing attacks exploit human psychology and often employ urgency or fear to manipulate victims into taking actions that compromise their security.

Social Engineering Attacks:

Social engineering attacks manipulate human behavior to deceive individuals into divulging sensitive information or performing actions that compromise security. Attackers may impersonate trusted individuals, exploit relationships, or use persuasive tactics to gain unauthorized access to systems or sensitive data. Common social engineering techniques include pretexting, baiting, tailgating, and impersonation.

Password Attacks:

Password attacks aim to gain unauthorized access to accounts by exploiting weak passwords or compromised login credentials. Cybercriminals use various methods such as brute-force attacks, dictionary attacks, and credential stuffing to guess or obtain passwords. Once compromised, passwords can provide attackers with access to sensitive data, personal accounts, or even privileged systems within organizations.

Denial-Of-Service (Dos) Attacks:

Denial-of-Service attacks disrupt or disable computer systems, networks, or websites by overwhelming them with a flood of traffic or resource requests. This renders the targeted service unavailable to legitimate users. Distributed Denial-of-Service (DDoS) attacks involve multiple compromised systems coordinated to launch an attack, amplifying its impact. DoS attacks can disrupt business operations, cause financial losses, or function as a smokescreen for other cybercriminal activities.

Insider Threats:

Insider threats refer to individuals within an organization who misuse their authorized access to compromise security. These threats can be intentional, such as disgruntled employees leaking sensitive information or sabotaging systems, or unintentional, such as employees falling victim to social engineering attacks. Insider threats pose significant risks to organizations, and implementing proper access controls, monitoring, and employee training is essential to mitigate these risks.

Unpatched Software Vulnerabilities:

Software vulnerabilities are weaknesses or flaws in software programs, operating systems, or applications that can be exploited by cybercriminals to gain unauthorized access or execute malicious code. Attackers actively scan for unpatched systems or zero-day vulnerabilities (unpublished vulnerabilities) to exploit. Regularly updating software and promptly applying security patches is crucial to minimize the risk of exploitation.

By understanding these common cybersecurity risks, individuals and organizations can better prepare and implement proactive security measures to protect themselves from potential threats. Vigilance, user education, and the use of robust security tools and practices are essential in mitigating these risks.

CHAPTER 3: PASSWORD SECURITY

The Importance of Strong Passwords

P asswords function as the first line of defense against unauthorized access to personal and sensitive information. Creating and using strong passwords is crucial to protect your accounts and maintain cybersecurity. Here's why strong passwords are important:

Preventing Unauthorized Access: Strong passwords make it significantly more difficult for cybercriminals to guess or crack them, reducing the risk of unauthorized access to your accounts and sensitive data.

Protecting Multiple Accounts: Using unique and strong passwords for each account ensures that a breach in one account does not compromise all your other accounts. Reusing passwords across multiple accounts increases the risk of a domino effect if one account is compromised.

Safeguarding Personal and Financial Information: Many online accounts store personal and financial information. A strong password helps protect this sensitive data from falling into the wrong hands, preventing identity theft, financial fraud, and other malicious activities.

Creating Strong Passwords

Creating strong passwords involves using a combination of elements that make it challenging for attackers to guess or crack them. Here are some tips for creating strong passwords:

Length: Use passwords that are at least 12 characters long. The longer the password, the more secure it is.

Complexity: Include a mix of uppercase and lowercase letters, numbers, and special characters in your password. Avoid using easily guessable patterns or dictionary words.

Avoid Personal Information: Don't use personal information such as your name, birthdate, or pet's name in your password, as this information can be easily obtained or guessed.

Passphrase Approach: Consider using a passphrase, which is a series of words or a sentence. Passphrases are easier to remember and can be more secure than traditional passwords if they are long and not easily guessable.

Avoid Common Passwords: Avoid using commonly used passwords, such as "123456," "password," or "qwerty." These passwords are easily guessable and frequently targeted by attackers.

Regularly Update Passwords: Change your passwords regularly, ideally every three to six months, to minimize the risk of unauthorized access even if a password breach occurs.

Password Management Tools

Managing strong and unique passwords for multiple accounts can be challenging. Password management tools can help simplify this process. Here is how they work:

Password Generators: Password management tools can generate strong, random passwords for you. These passwords are complex and highly secure, reducing the risk of compromise.

Secure Storage: Password management tools securely store your passwords in an encrypted database. This eliminates the need to remember multiple passwords while keeping them protected.

Auto-Fill Functionality: Many password managers offer auto-fill features, allowing you to automatically populate login credentials when accessing websites or applications.

Synchronization Across Devices: Password managers often provide synchronization across multiple devices, enabling you to access your passwords securely from different platforms.

The Role of Password Managers

Password managers are powerful tools for enhancing password security and simplifying password management. Here are some benefits of using password managers:

Strong and Unique Passwords: Password managers generate and store strong, unique passwords for each account, eliminating the need to remember them.

Convenient Access: With a password manager, you only need to remember one primary password to access all your stored passwords, making it more convenient and secure.

Encrypted Storage: Password managers encrypt your password database, ensuring that even if it is compromised, the passwords remain protected.

Security Alerts: Some password managers provide security alerts that notify you if any of your stored accounts are involved in a data breach or if any passwords are weak or compromised.

Enhanced Authentication: Password managers often offer additional security features, such as two-factor authentication.

CHAPTER 4: TWO-FACTOR AUTHENTICATION (2FA)

Understanding Two-Factor Authentication (2FA)

Two-Factor Authentication (2FA) is an additional layer of security that provides an extra level of protection beyond passwords. It adds a second step to the authentication process, making it more challenging for attackers to gain unauthorized access to your accounts. 2FA requires users to provide two or more forms of verification, typically something they know (password), something they have (e.g., a smartphone or security token), or something they are (biometric data). By combining multiple factors, 2FA significantly strengthens the security of your accounts.

How Two-Factor Authentication Works

The process of 2FA typically involves the following steps:

Step 1: Username and Password: You enter your username and password as the first factor during the login process.

Step 2: Second Authentication Factor: After entering your credentials, you are prompted to provide the second factor. This can be in the form of a verification code sent via SMS, a generated code from an authentication app, a physical security token, or a biometric scan (fingerprint, facial recognition, etc.).

Step 3: Authentication Verification: Once you provide the second factor, it is validated by the service provider to verify your identity. If the second factor is successfully authenticated, access to your account is granted.

Benefits of Two-Factor Authentication

Implementing 2FA offers several benefits in terms of enhancing security and protecting your accounts:

Increased Security: 2FA significantly reduces the risk of unauthorized access, even if an attacker manages to obtain or crack your password. The second factor acts as an additional barrier, making it much harder for attackers to breach your accounts.

Mitigation of Password Vulnerabilities: Since passwords alone can be vulnerable to various attacks, 2FA provides an extra layer of protection, reducing the impact of password-related risks.

Protection against Credential Theft: In cases where passwords are compromised through data breaches or phishing attacks, 2FA prevents attackers from accessing your accounts without the second factor.

Peace of Mind: By enabling 2FA, you gain peace of mind knowing that your accounts have an added layer of security, reducing the chances of falling victim to cybercriminals.

Implementing Two-Factor Authentication

To leverage the benefits of 2FA effectively, follow these best practices for implementation:

Enable 2FA for Critical Accounts: Enable 2FA for all accounts that contain sensitive personal or financial information, such as email, online banking, social media, and cloud storage accounts.

Use App-Based Authentication: Whenever possible, opt for app-based 2FA methods over SMS-based methods. Authentication apps generate time-based one-time passwords (TOTPs) that are more secure than SMS codes, which can be intercepted.

Backup and Recovery: Set up backup options and ensure you have a recovery process in place in case you lose access to your second-factor device or forget your backup codes.

Periodically Review and Update: Regularly review your accounts and ensure that 2FA is enabled where available. Keep the authentication apps, recovery options, and contact information up to date.

Educate and Encourage Others: Spread awareness about the importance of 2FA and encourage friends, family, and colleagues to adopt it for their accounts.

CHAPTER 5: EMAIL SECURITY AND PHISHING AWARENESS

What is Phishing?

P hishing is a form of cyber-attack where an attacker masquerades as a trustworthy entity to trick individuals into revealing sensitive information, such as passwords, credit card details, or social security numbers. The term "phishing" is derived from the analogy of fishing, where attackers cast a wide net in hopes of catching unsuspecting victims.

Phishing attacks commonly occur through email, although they can also happen through other communication channels like text messages, social media, or instant messaging platforms. The attackers typically employ social engineering techniques to manipulate their targets into taking a desired action, such as clicking on a malicious link, downloading an infected attachment, or providing personal information.

Here is an Overview of Common Phishing Techniques:

Email Spoofing: Attackers forge the sender's email address to make it appear as if the email is coming from a legitimate source, such as a well-known company or a trusted individual.

Deceptive URLs: Phishing emails often contain links that direct users to fraudulent websites that mimic legitimate ones. These websites are designed to collect login credentials or financial information.

Spear Phishing: In spear phishing attacks, the attackers personalize their messages and tailor them to specific individuals or organizations. They gather information from various sources to make their emails appear more convincing and increase the likelihood of success.

Smishing: Smishing is a type of phishing that occurs through SMS text messages. Attackers send deceptive messages with links or phone numbers, attempting to trick recipients into providing sensitive information or calling a fraudulent number.

Vishing: Vishing, or voice phishing, involves attackers using voice communication, typically over the phone, to deceive individuals into revealing personal information or performing certain actions.

Phishing attacks can have severe consequences, including financial loss, identity theft, and compromised systems or networks. To protect against phishing attacks, it is important to be vigilant, exercise caution when interacting with emails or messages, and follow best practices such as not clicking on suspicious links, verifying the authenticity of messages, and keeping software and security tools up to date.

Recognizing Phishing Emails

Recognizing phishing emails is crucial to protect yourself from falling victim to these deceptive attacks. Here are some tips to help you identify phishing emails:

Sender's Email Address: Check the email address of the sender. Phishing emails often use email addresses that are slightly altered or mimic legitimate ones. Look for misspellings, additional numbers or characters, or unusual domain names.

Generic Greetings or Salutations: Phishing emails often use generic greetings like "Dear Customer" or "Dear User" instead of addressing you by your name. Legitimate emails from trusted organizations usually address you personally.

Urgent or Threatening Language: Phishing emails may try to create a sense of urgency or fear to prompt immediate action. Be cautious of emails that threaten consequences, claim account suspension, or urge you to take urgent action without proper context.

Poor Grammar and Spelling Mistakes: Phishing emails often contain grammatical errors, typos, and awkward sentence structures. Legitimate organizations typically have professional communication standards, so be wary of poorly written emails.

Suspicious Attachments or Links: Be cautious of attachments or links in emails from unknown or unexpected sources. Hover your mouse over links (without clicking) to check if the URL matches the displayed text. Be wary of shortened URLs or URLs that look slightly different from the official website.

Request for Personal or Financial Information: Phishing emails often request sensitive information like passwords, social security numbers, or credit card details. Legitimate organizations usually do not ask for such information via email.

Unexpected Requests or Offers: Be cautious of emails promising unexpected rewards, prizes, or offers that seem too good to be true. These could be phishing attempts to lure you into providing personal information or clicking on malicious links.

Requests for Money or Gift Cards: Phishing emails may ask for money transfers or request you to purchase gift cards and provide the codes. Legitimate organizations typically do not ask for financial assistance through email.

Suspicious or Poorly Designed Email Layout: Phishing emails may have inconsistent formatting, mismatched logos, or low-quality graphics. Be cautious if the email does not match the usual style and design of the organization's official communications.

Trust Your Instincts: If something feels off or suspicious about an email, trust your instincts. It is better to err on the side of caution and verify the legitimacy of the email through alternative means, such as contacting the organization directly.

Remember, cybercriminals are continually evolving their tactics, so it is essential to stay informed, be cautious, and rely on your judgment when assessing the legitimacy of an email. If you suspect an email to be a phishing attempt, it is best to report it to your organization's IT department or the relevant authorities.

Protecting Yourself from

Phishing Attacks

Protecting yourself from phishing attacks is crucial to safeguard your personal information and digital security. Here are some essential steps you can take to protect yourself:

Develop A Security Mindset:

Be Skeptical: Approach every email, message, or communication with a healthy level of skepticism, especially if it asks for personal or sensitive information.

Think Before you Act: Pause and carefully consider any requests or actions before taking them. Phishing attacks often create a sense of urgency to prompt impulsive responses. Take your time and verify the legitimacy of the request.

Verify the Sender: Check the email address: Examine the sender's email address closely for any signs of alteration or suspicious domains. Be cautious of emails that claim to be from well-known organizations but have unusual or misspelled email addresses.

Cross-reference with Official Sources: If you receive an email from a company or organization, verify its legitimacy by independently searching for their contact information and comparing it with the information in the email.

Be Wary of Links and Attachments: Hover before you click: Hover your mouse over links to preview the URL before clicking. Ensure that the URL matches the displayed text and appears legitimate.

Avoid Downloading Suspicious Attachments: Be cautious when opening attachments, especially from unknown senders. Malicious attachments can contain malware that compromises your system. Scan attachments with security software before opening them.

Implement Security Measures: Use reputable security software:

Install and regularly update reliable antivirus and anti-malware software to detect and block phishing attempts and other malicious activities.

Enable Multi-Factor Authentication (MFA): Enable MFA whenever possible, as it adds an extra layer of security to your accounts by requiring additional verification, such as a unique code or biometric authentication.

Keep your Devices Updated: Keep your operating system, web browsers, and other software up to date with the latest security patches and updates. These updates often include important security fixes.

Educate Yourself: Stay informed: Stay updated on the latest phishing techniques and trends. Subscribe to reputable cybersecurity blogs, follow security experts on social media, and read security news to enhance your awareness.

Learn to Spot Phishing Indicators: Familiarize yourself with common phishing indicators such as misspellings, grammatical errors, generic greetings, urgent language, and requests for personal or financial information.

Report and Block: Report phishing attempts: If you receive a phishing email, report it to your organization's IT department, the legitimate organization being impersonated, or your email provider. Reporting helps raise awareness and assists in taking appropriate action.

Block and Mark as Spam: Use the spam or junk mail feature in your email client to block future emails from suspicious senders. This helps reduce the likelihood of phishing emails reaching your inbox.

Remember, no security measure is foolproof, and attackers are constantly evolving their tactics. By adopting these practices, staying vigilant, and continuously educating yourself, you can significantly reduce the risk of falling victim to phishing attacks.

The Importance of Email Security

Email is a widely used communication medium, making it a common target for cybercriminals. Protecting your email accounts is crucial to prevent unauthorized access, data breaches, and phishing attacks. Here's why email security is important:

Confidentiality: Emails often contain sensitive information, including personal details, financial data, or business communications. Proper email security safeguards the confidentiality of this information.

Identity Protection: Email accounts are frequently used for account verification, password resets, and communication with various online services. Securing your email helps protect your online identity and prevents unauthorized access to other accounts.

Phishing Prevention: Cybercriminals commonly use email as a medium for phishing attacks, attempting to trick users into revealing sensitive information. Strong email security practices help identify and mitigate such threats.

Email Security Best Practices

Implementing strong email security practices is crucial to protect yourself from phishing attacks and maintain the confidentiality of your information. Consider the following best practices:

Use Strong Passwords: Create unique, complex passwords for your email accounts. Follow the guidelines provided in Chapter 3 on password security.

Enable Two-Factor Authentication (2FA): Enable 2FA for your email accounts to add an extra layer of security.

Be Cautious of Links and Attachments: Avoid clicking on suspicious links or opening email attachments from unknown sources. Verify the legitimacy of the sender and scan attachments for malware before opening them.

Keep Software Updated: Ensure that your email client and antivirus software are up to date to protect against known vulnerabilities and emerging threats.

Regularly Monitor and Review Emails: Regularly review your inbox and spam folder to identify potential phishing emails. Flag suspicious messages and report them to your email provider.

Educate Yourself: Stay informed about the latest phishing techniques and common scams. Educate yourself on how to identify phishing emails and share this knowledge with others.

CHAPTER 6: SECURE WEB BROWSING PRACTICES

Importance of Secure Web Browsing

Web browsing is a primary activity for most individuals, but it exposes users to various online threats. Adhering to secure web browsing practices is essential to protect against malware infections, data breaches, and unauthorized access. Here's why secure web browsing matters:

Malware Protection: Secure web browsing practices help mitigate the risk of inadvertently downloading malware from infected websites or malicious advertisements.

Data Privacy: Protecting your web browsing activity helps safeguard your personal information, preventing unauthorized tracking, profiling, or data collection by third parties.

Avoiding Phishing Attacks: Secure web browsing practices reduce the chances of falling victim to phishing attacks by being cautious of suspicious websites and verifying the legitimacy of the websites you visit.

Preventing Identity Theft: Secure web browsing minimizes the risk of identity theft by protecting your login credentials, financial information, and other sensitive data from being intercepted or stolen.

Secure Web Browsing Best Practices

To ensure a secure web browsing experience, consider implementing the following best practices:

Keep Your Browser Updated: Regularly update your web browser to the latest version, as updates often include security patches that address vulnerabilities.

Use a Secure Connection: Access websites over a secure connection by ensuring that the website address begins with "https://". The "s" indicates that the connection is encrypted, providing a higher level of security.

Be Wary of Untrusted Websites: Avoid visiting suspicious websites that may host malware or engage in phishing activities. Stick to reputable sources and be cautious when clicking on links from unfamiliar sources.

Utilize Ad and Script Blockers: Install ad blockers and script blockers to reduce the risk of malicious advertisements and scripts running on websites. These tools can help prevent malware infections and drive-by downloads.

Exercise Caution with Downloads: Be cautious when downloading files from the internet. Only download files from trusted sources and scan them with antivirus software before opening or executing them.

Disable Autofill and Form Saving: Disable the autofill feature in your browser and avoid saving sensitive information in forms, such as passwords or credit card details. This reduces the risk of unauthorized access to your personal information.

Clear Your Browsing Data: Regularly clear your browsing history, cookies, and cached data. This helps protect your privacy and minimizes the risk of unauthorized access to your browsing habits and stored information.

Implement Web Security Extensions: Install reputable web security extensions that provide additional layers of protection, such as blocking malicious websites, protecting against phishing attempts, and warning about potentially harmful downloads.

Public Wi-Fi Security

Introduction To Public Wi-Fi Security

Public Wi-Fi networks are convenient for staying connected on the go, but they can also pose significant security risks. Without proper precautions, using public Wi-Fi can expose your personal information to cybercriminals who may be lurking on the same network. In this chapter, we will explore essential tips and best practices to protect your privacy and security when using public Wi-Fi.

Understanding the Risks

When connecting to public Wi-Fi networks, you expose yourself to various risks, including:

Man-in-the-Middle Attacks: Cybercriminals can intercept and eavesdrop on the data transmitted between your device and the network, potentially gaining access to sensitive information such as passwords, financial details, or personal communications.

Malware Distribution: Public Wi-Fi networks can be a breeding ground for malware. Attackers can inject malicious software into the network or create fake networks to distribute malware-infected files to unsuspecting users.

Rogue Networks: Attackers can create fake Wi-Fi networks with names that appear similar to legitimate networks to trick users into connecting to them. Once connected, attackers can monitor your online activities or launch attacks on your device.

Snooping and Data Theft: Cybercriminals can use specialized tools to intercept your unencrypted data, including usernames, passwords, and credit card information, as it travels over the network.

Public Wi-Fi Security Best Practices

To protect yourself when using public Wi-Fi, follow these best practices:

Use Trusted Networks: Whenever possible, connect to trusted networks such as those provided by reputable establishments like hotels, cafes, or airports. These networks are more likely to have implemented security measures.

Verify Network Authenticity: Confirm the correct network name with the establishment or staff before connecting. Be cautious of networks with generic names like "Free Wi-Fi" or variations that may indicate a rogue network.

Connect to Encrypted Networks: Look for networks that require a password or use encryption, such as WPA2 or WPA3. Encrypted networks add an additional layer of security by encrypting your data transmission.

Use a Virtual Private Network (VPN): A VPN creates a secure and encrypted connection between your device and the internet, even on public Wi-Fi networks. Use a reputable VPN service to protect your data from interception and maintain your privacy.

Disable Auto-Connect and Wi-Fi Sharing: Turn off the automatic connection feature on your device to prevent it from connecting to unknown networks without your consent. Similarly, avoid sharing your Wi-Fi connection with others to maintain control over your network security.

Limit Sensitive Activities: Avoid performing sensitive activities, such as online banking or accessing confidential accounts, while connected to public Wi-Fi. Wait until you are on a trusted network or use cellular data instead.

Enable Firewall and Antivirus Protection: Ensure that your device's firewall is enabled and keep your antivirus software up to date. These security measures can help detect and block malicious activities.

Use HTTPS and SSL/TLS: Whenever possible, ensure the websites you visit use HTTPS (Hypertext Transfer Protocol Secure) and have a valid SSL/TLS certificate. HTTPS encrypts your data transmission, making it harder for attackers to intercept.

Disable File Sharing and AirDrop: Disable file sharing features on your device to prevent unauthorized access to your files or data. Similarly, turn off AirDrop or set it to "Contacts Only" to avoid unwanted file sharing requests.

Monitor for Suspicious Activity: Regularly check your device for any signs of unusual behavior, such as unexpected pop-ups, slow performance, or unauthorized access attempts. These could indicate a security breach.

CHAPTER 7: MOBILE DEVICE SECURITY

Importance of Mobile Device Security

Mobile devices, such as smartphones and tablets, have become an integral part of our lives. They store sensitive personal information, provide access to online services, and are vulnerable to various security threats. Ensuring mobile device security is vital to protect your privacy, data, and online accounts. Here's why mobile device security matters:

Data Protection: Mobile devices store personal information, including contacts, messages, emails, photos, and financial data. Securing your mobile device protects this data from unauthorized access or loss.

Secure Communication: Mobile devices are used for messaging, calls, and accessing online services. Ensuring mobile device security safeguards your communications and protects against eavesdropping or interception.

App Security: Mobile devices rely on apps for various tasks, including banking, social media, and email. Mobile device security prevents malicious apps from compromising your data or stealing sensitive information.

Online Account Protection: Mobile devices often have apps that provide access to your online accounts. Securing your mobile device reduces the risk of unauthorized access to these accounts.

Securing Your Mobile Device

To enhance the security of your mobile devices, consider implementing the following best practices:

Enable Device Lock: Set up a PIN, password, pattern, or biometric authentication (e.g., fingerprint or face recognition) to lock your device. This protects your data in case of loss or theft.

Keep Software Updated: Regularly update your mobile device's operating system and apps to ensure you have the latest security patches and bug fixes.

Install Apps from Trusted Sources: Download apps only from official app stores, such as Google Play Store (Android) or Apple App Store (iOS). Avoid downloading apps from third-party sources, as they may contain malware or malicious code.

Review App Permissions: When installing apps, carefully review the permissions they request. Grant permissions only if they are necessary for the app's functionality. Be cautious of apps that request excessive permissions that seem unrelated to their purpose.

Use App Lock and Encryption: Enable app lock features or use third-party app lockers to secure sensitive apps with an additional layer of authentication. Additionally, consider encrypting your device's storage to protect your data if the device is lost or stolen.

Be Cautious of Public Wi-Fi: Avoid accessing sensitive information or conducting financial transactions while connected to public Wi-Fi networks. Use a virtual private network (VPN) when connecting to public Wi-Fi to encrypt your internet traffic and enhance security.

Enable Find My Device: Activate the "Find My Device" or similar feature on your mobile device. This allows you to track your device's location, remotely lock or wipe its data, and increase the chances of recovering a lost or stolen device.

Regularly Backup Your Data: Back up your mobile device's data regularly to an external storage device or a cloud service. This ensures that even if your device is compromised or lost, you can restore your important data.

Mobile Device Theft and Loss Prevention

Introduction To Mobile Device Theft And Loss

Mobile devices, such as smartphones and tablets, are highly valuable and attractive targets for thieves. In addition to the monetary value, these devices often contain sensitive personal information, making their theft or loss a significant security concern. This chapter will explore strategies to prevent mobile device theft and mitigate the impact of loss.

Physical Security Measures

Implementing physical security measures can help protect your mobile device from theft and minimize the risk of loss. Consider the following practices:

Keep your Device Secure: Use passcodes or biometric authentication (e.g., fingerprint or face recognition) to lock your device. This prevents unauthorized access and ensures that your data remains protected.

Enable Device Tracking Features: Such as Find My iPhone (iOS) or Find My Device (Android). These services can help locate and remotely lock or erase your device in case of theft or loss.

Avoid Leaving your Device Unattended: In public places, such as restaurants, airports, or public transportation. Keep it within sight or secured in a bag or pocket.

Be Mindful in Crowded Areas: Stay alert in crowded areas where thefts are more likely to occur. Keep a firm grip on your device and remain aware of your surroundings.

Use Physical Security Accessories: Consider using a sturdy case or protective cover for your device, which can provide some resistance against physical damage and make it less attractive to thieves.

Invest in a Secure Lock or Tethering System: to secure your device when using it in public spaces. These accessories can prevent opportunistic thefts.

Data Protection and Remote Wiping

Protecting the data stored on your mobile device is crucial in the event of theft or loss. By implementing the following practices, you can mitigate the risk of unauthorized access to your personal information:

Enable Device Encryption: Encrypt your device's storage to ensure that your data is protected even if the device falls into the wrong hands. This feature is available on most modern smartphones and tablets.

Regularly Back Up Your Data: Create regular backups of your device's data to a secure location, such as a cloud storage service or a computer. This ensures that even if your device is lost or stolen, you can still access your valuable information.

Enable Remote Wiping: Configure your device to allow remote wiping in case of theft or loss. This feature enables you to erase all data on your device remotely, ensuring that your personal information remains protected.

Theft and Loss Recovery

In the unfortunate event that your mobile device is stolen or lost, there are steps you can take to increase the chances of recovery:

Report The Incident: Immediately report the theft or loss to the local authorities. Provide them with all relevant details, including the device's make, model, serial number, and any unique identifiers.

Notify Your Service Provider: Contact your mobile service provider to report the theft or loss. They can assist in suspending or deactivating your SIM card to prevent unauthorized usage.

Change Passwords and Notify Financial Institutions: Change the passwords for your email accounts, social media accounts, and any other apps or services linked to your mobile device. Notify your bank and credit card companies about the incident to ensure they monitor for any suspicious activity.

Track and Locate Your Device: If you have enabled device tracking features, use them to track the location of your device. Provide this information to the authorities to aid in recovery.

CHAPTER 8: SOCIAL MEDIA SECURITY

Risks of Social Media

S ocial media platforms have revolutionized the way we connect, share, and interact online. However, they also present certain risks that can compromise our privacy and security. In this chapter, we will explore the risks associated with social media and strategies to enhance your social media security.

Securing Your Social Media Accounts

Securing your social media accounts is essential to protect your personal information and prevent unauthorized access. Follow these best practices to enhance the security of your social media accounts:

Use Strong, Unique Passwords: Create strong, complex passwords for each social media account. Avoid using easily guessable information such as your name or birthdate. Consider using a password manager to securely store and manage your passwords.

Enable Two-Factor Authentication (2FA): Activate 2FA on your social media accounts whenever possible. This adds an extra layer of security by requiring a second form of verification, such as a unique code sent to your mobile device, in addition to your password.

Be Cautious of Third-Party Apps and Permissions: Review and manage the permissions granted to third-party apps connected to your social media accounts. Remove any unnecessary or suspicious apps and regularly review the access levels of authorized apps.

Regularly Update Your Account Settings: Periodically review and update your account settings to ensure they align with your desired level of privacy and security. Pay attention to options related to visibility, post sharing, tagging, and data collection.

Privacy Settings and Sharing Safely

Understanding and utilizing privacy settings is crucial to control the visibility of your social media content and protect your privacy. Consider the following recommendations:

Review Privacy Settings: Familiarize yourself with the privacy settings of each social media platform you use. Customize your settings to limit the visibility of your posts and personal information to only trusted connections.

Be Mindful of What you Share: Exercise caution when sharing personal information on social media. Avoid sharing sensitive details such as your home address, phone number, or financial information. Consider the potential consequences before posting any content.

Limit Public Visibility: Adjust the visibility of your posts to limit them to your trusted connections rather than making them public. Avoid sharing intimate details or compromising photos that could be misused or exploited.

Control Photo and Tag Settings: Manage settings related to photo tagging and facial recognition features. Choose whether you want to be tagged in photos automatically and review tags before they appear on your profile.

Recognizing and Reporting Cyberbullying

Cyberbullying is a significant issue on social media platforms that can have detrimental effects on individuals' mental well-being. Learn to recognize and respond to cyberbullying incidents:

Familiarize Yourself with Cyberbullying Indicators: Be aware of signs of cyberbullying, such as abusive or threatening messages, spreading rumors or lies, impersonation, or targeted harassment.

Report and Block Offenders: If you experience or witness cyberbullying, report the incidents to the social media platform. Most platforms have reporting mechanisms in place to address such issues. Consider blocking the individuals involved to prevent further interactions.

Preserve Evidence: Take screenshots or save any evidence of cyberbullying incidents. This documentation can support your case when reporting the issue and can be useful if legal action is necessary.

Seek Support: Reach out to trusted friends, family, or professionals if you are a victim of cyberbullying. They can provide guidance, support, and help you navigate the situation.

Remember, maintaining a safe and secure social media presence requires ongoing vigilance. Regularly review and update your privacy settings, be mindful of what you share, and promptly report any suspicious or harmful activities to ensure a positive social media experience.

CHAPTER 9: HOME NETWORK SECURITY

Securing Your Home Wi-Fi Network

Y our home Wi-Fi network is the gateway to the internet for all your connected devices. It is crucial to secure it properly to protect your personal information and prevent unauthorized access. Follow these steps to secure your home Wi-Fi network:

Change the Default Network Name (SSID): Modify the default network name of your Wi-Fi network to a unique and non-identifying name. This prevents attackers from easily identifying the type of router you are using.

Set a Strong Wi-Fi Password: Create a strong and complex password for your Wi-Fi network. Use a combination of upper and lowercase letters, numbers, and special characters. Avoid using easily guessable information such as your name or address.

Enable Wi-Fi Network Encryption: Enable WPA2 (Wi-Fi Protected Access 2) or WPA3 encryption on your Wi-Fi network. These encryption protocols ensure that data transmitted between your devices and the router is secure and protected from eavesdropping.

Disable Wi-Fi Protected Setup (WPS): WPS is a feature that simplifies the process of connecting devices to your Wi-Fi network. However, it can also be exploited by attackers to gain unauthorized access. Disable WPS on your router to enhance security.

Router Security Best Practices

The router is the central device that connects your home network to the internet. Implement these best practices to enhance router security:

Change the Default Administrator Credentials: Most routers come with default administrator usernames and passwords. Change these credentials to unique and strong values to prevent unauthorized access to your router's settings.

Disable Remote Administration: Disable the option for remote administration on your router. This ensures that only devices connected to your home network can access the router's settings.

Enable Router Firewall: Enable the built-in firewall on your router to filter incoming and outgoing network traffic. This adds an extra layer of protection against unauthorized access and potential threats.

Disable UPnP (Universal Plug and Play): UPnP is a feature that allows devices on your network to automatically configure router settings. However, it can also be exploited by attackers. Disable UPnP unless you specifically require it.

Network Firewall and Intrusion Detection Systems

Implementing network-level security measures such as a firewall and intrusion detection systems (IDS) adds an extra layer of protection to your home network:

Set Up a Network Firewall: Install a network firewall to monitor and control incoming and outgoing network traffic. A firewall can help block unauthorized access attempts and filter out malicious traffic.

Consider an Intrusion Detection System (IDS): An IDS monitors network traffic for signs of suspicious or malicious activity. It can detect and alert you about potential attacks, allowing you to take necessary actions to mitigate the risks.

Keep Firewall and IDS Software up to Date: Regularly update the firmware and software of your firewall and IDS to ensure they have the latest security patches and features.

Regular Software Updates

Regularly updating the software and firmware of your devices is crucial to maintaining their security. This includes your router, connected devices, and any additional network security tools you use. Follow these practices:

Keep Router Firmware up to Date: Check for firmware updates from your router manufacturer and apply them promptly. Firmware updates often include security patches and bug fixes that address vulnerabilities.

Update Connected Devices: Regularly update the operating systems, firmware, and applications on all your connected devices. These updates often contain security enhancements and patches for known vulnerabilities.

Enable Automatic Updates: Whenever possible, enable automatic updates on your devices. This ensures that you receive the latest security updates without manual intervention.

By securing your home Wi-Fi network, implementing router security best practices, utilizing network-level security tools, and keeping software up to date, individuals can significantly strengthen the security of their home network and protect against potential threats.

CHAPTER 10: DATA BACKUP AND RECOVERY

The Importance of Data Backup

D ata backup is a critical aspect of cybersecurity and data protection. Accidental file deletion, hardware failure, malware attacks, or natural disasters can result in data loss. Understanding the importance of data backup is essential for ensuring the continuity of your personal and business operations. This chapter explores the significance of data backup and recovery.

Choosing the Right Backup Solution

Selecting the appropriate backup solution is crucial for effective data protection. Consider the following factors when choosing a backup solution:

Backup Type: Decide between local backups, cloud backups, or a combination of both. Local backups provide immediate access and control over your data, while cloud backups offer offsite storage and protection against physical disasters.

Storage Capacity: Determine the amount of storage required to accommodate your data backup needs. Consider the growth of your data over time and choose a solution that can scale accordingly.

Security Measures: Ensure that the backup solution incorporates robust security measures to protect your data during storage and transmission. Encryption, access controls, and data integrity mechanisms are essential for maintaining the confidentiality and integrity of your backups.

Automation and Scheduling: Look for backup solutions that offer automation and scheduling features. This enables regular and consistent backups without manual intervention, reducing the risk of data loss.

Implementing a Backup Strategy

Developing a backup strategy is essential for ensuring comprehensive data protection. Follow these steps to implement an effective backup strategy:

Identify Critical Data: Determine which data is critical for your personal or business operations. Focus on files and information that, if lost, would have a significant impact on your productivity or cause irreparable harm.

Define Backup Frequency: Decide how often you need to perform backups based on the frequency of data changes and the importance of the information. Critical data may require daily backups, while less critical data can be backed up less frequently.

Select Backup Locations: Determine where your backups will be stored. This can include external hard drives, network-attached storage (NAS) devices, cloud storage services, or a combination of these options.

Test and Validate Backups: Regularly test your backups to ensure they are functioning correctly. Perform restoration tests to verify that you can retrieve your data successfully. Regular testing helps identify any issues or errors in the backup process before they become critical.

Data Recovery Methods

In the event of data loss, having reliable data recovery methods can help restore your information and minimize the impact. Consider the following data recovery methods:

Restore from Local Backup: If you have local backups, you can restore your data directly from the backup storage device. Connect the backup device to the affected system and follow the restore process provided by your backup solution.

Retrieve from Cloud Backup: If you have cloud backups, access the backup service, and follow the instructions to restore your data. This may involve selecting specific files or folders to recover or initiating a complete system restore.

Data Recovery Software: In some cases, data recovery software can help retrieve lost or deleted files from storage devices, even without a comprehensive backup. These tools scan the storage media for recoverable data and provide options for restoration.

Professional Data Recovery Services: If your data loss is due to severe hardware failure or physical damage, professional data recovery services may be required. These specialized services can attempt to recover data from damaged storage devices in a controlled environment.

Remember to regularly review and update your backup strategy as your data storage needs evolve. Conduct periodic tests of your backups and ensure that recovery methods are documented and easily accessible. By implementing a robust backup strategy and understanding data recovery methods, you can safeguard your valuable information and mitigate the risks of data loss.

CHAPTER 11: SAFE ONLINE SHOPPING AND BANKING

Secure Online Shopping Practices

Online shopping offers convenience and accessibility, but it also comes with certain risks. Safeguard your personal and financial information by following these secure online shopping practices:

Shop from Trusted Websites: Only make purchases from reputable and well-known online retailers. Look for secure website indicators such as a padlock symbol in the address bar or "https" in the URL, indicating a secure connection.

Use Secure Payment Methods: Opt for secure payment options such as credit cards or trusted payment gateways. These methods offer additional fraud protection and allow you to dispute unauthorized charges.

Be Cautious with Personal Information: Avoid sharing unnecessary personal information during the checkout process. Legitimate online retailers typically do not require extensive personal details beyond what is necessary to complete the transaction.

Keep Devices and Software Updated: Regularly update your devices and web browsers with the latest security patches and software updates. Outdated software may have vulnerabilities that can be exploited by attackers.

Protecting Your Financial Information

Protecting your financial information is crucial to prevent unauthorized access and fraudulent activities. Follow these measures to safeguard your financial data:

Use Strong and Unique Passwords: Create strong, complex passwords for your financial accounts and avoid reusing passwords across different platforms. Consider using a password manager to securely store and manage your passwords.

Enable Two-Factor Authentication (2FA): Activate 2FA for your online banking and financial accounts whenever possible. This adds an extra layer of security by requiring a second form of verification, such as a unique code sent to your mobile device, in addition to your password.

Regularly Monitor your Accounts: Keep a close eye on your financial transactions and statements. Report any suspicious or unauthorized activities to your bank or financial institution immediately.

Be Cautious with Financial Emails and Communications: Exercise caution when responding to emails or messages requesting your financial information. Avoid clicking on links or downloading attachments from unknown or suspicious sources.

Online Banking Security Measures

Online banking provides convenience, but it requires robust security measures to protect your financial information. Consider these online banking security practices:

Use a Secure and Private Network: Access your online banking only from trusted networks, preferably using a private and encrypted Wi-Fi connection. Public Wi-Fi networks are more susceptible to eavesdropping and data interception.

Enable Transaction Notifications: Set up transaction notifications or alerts provided by your bank. This allows you to receive real-time alerts for any financial activities, helping you detect and respond to suspicious transactions promptly.

Regularly Review Account Activity: Monitor your online banking transactions regularly. Review your account statements and check for any discrepancies or unfamiliar transactions. Report any issues to your bank immediately.

Keep your Banking App and Devices Secure: Install the official banking app from your bank's trusted source (e.g., official app stores). Keep the app and your devices updated with the latest security patches. Enable biometric authentication, such as fingerprint or face recognition, for added security.

Recognizing and Reporting Financial Scams

Financial scams are prevalent online, targeting unsuspecting individuals for fraudulent purposes. Learn to recognize and report financial scams to protect yourself and others:

Be Cautious of Unsolicited Communications: Be skeptical of unsolicited emails, phone calls, or messages claiming to be from banks or financial institutions. Legitimate organizations typically do not request sensitive information through such channels.

Verify the Source: Before providing any financial information or making transactions, independently verify the authenticity of the source. Use official contact information obtained from trusted sources, such as your bank's official website or customer service hotline.

Educate Yourself About Common Scams: Stay informed about common financial scams, such as phishing, identity theft, or advance-fee fraud.

CHAPTER 12: EMPLOYEE CYBERSECURITY TRAINING

Cybersecurity Awareness for Employees

Cybersecurity awareness is essential for all employees to protect themselves and their organization from cyber threats. This chapter highlights the importance of cybersecurity awareness and provides guidance on educating employees about potential risks and best practices.

Understanding the Threat Landscape: Educate employees about the current cybersecurity landscape, including common threats such as phishing, malware, and social engineering attacks. Help them recognize the signs of potential threats and understand the consequences of security breaches.

Password Hygiene: Teach employees about the importance of strong and unique passwords, as well as the risks associated with password reuse. Encourage the use of password managers and the practice of regularly updating passwords.

Email Security: Train employees to identify suspicious emails, including phishing attempts and malicious attachments. Provide guidelines on how to handle suspicious emails, such as not clicking on unknown links or downloading suspicious attachments.

Social Engineering Awareness: Raise awareness about social engineering techniques used by attackers, such as pretexting, baiting, or impersonation. Teach employees to be cautious when sharing sensitive information or responding to requests from unknown or unverified sources.

Creating a Security Culture in the Workplace

Establishing a security culture within the workplace is crucial for maintaining a strong cybersecurity posture. Foster a security-conscious environment with the following practices:

Leadership Commitment: Ensure that organizational leaders prioritize cybersecurity and actively demonstrate their commitment to security practices. When leaders prioritize security, it sets a positive example for employees to follow.

Clear Security Policies and Guidelines: Develop comprehensive security policies and guidelines that outline acceptable use of technology, data protection protocols, and the consequences of non-compliance. Regularly communicate and reinforce these policies to employees.

Employee Training Programs: Implement regular cybersecurity training programs for employees to enhance their knowledge and skills. These programs can include workshops, online courses, or simulated phishing exercises to reinforce good security practices.

Encouraging Employee Engagement: Foster a culture of open communication and encourage employees to report any security concerns or incidents promptly. Establish channels for reporting, such as a dedicated email address or an anonymous reporting system.

Importance of Regular

Training and Updates

Cyber threats and attack techniques evolve rapidly, making regular training and updates crucial for maintaining strong cybersecurity practices. Emphasize the importance of ongoing training and updates with the following measures:

Continuous Education: Offer periodic cybersecurity training sessions to refresh employees' knowledge and introduce new security measures. Provide resources such as articles, videos, or webinars to keep employees informed about emerging threats and best practices.

Stay Updated with Industry Trends: Stay current with industry trends and new cybersecurity technologies. Share relevant information with employees to ensure they are aware of the latest security measures and can adapt to new challenges.

Tailor Training to Job Roles: Customize training programs to address the specific security concerns and responsibilities of different job roles within the organization. For example, IT staff may require specialized training on network security, while non-technical employees may need guidance on secure browsing and data handling.

Reinforce Training Through Regular Reminders: Send periodic reminders and tips to employees to reinforce cybersecurity best practices. These reminders can be in the form of email updates, posters, or internal newsletters, focusing on specific topics or seasonal security concerns.

CHAPTER 13: SECURING INTERNET OF THINGS (IOT) DEVICES

Understanding IoT Devices and Risks

The proliferation of Internet of Things (IoT) devices has brought numerous conveniences and functionalities to our lives. However, it has also introduced new security risks. This chapter explores the nature of IoT devices and the associated risks:

IoT Device Ecosystem: Understand the concept of IoT devices and their interconnected nature. IoT devices encompass a wide range of devices, from smart home appliances to wearables and industrial equipment, all connected to the internet.

Risks and Vulnerabilities: Explore the potential risks and vulnerabilities associated with IoT devices. These may include weak authentication mechanisms, outdated firmware, unencrypted communication, and lack of proper security controls.

Threats to Privacy and Data Security: Recognize the privacy implications and potential risks to personal data that can arise from IoT devices. Understand how the collection and processing of sensitive information by IoT devices can compromise privacy if not adequately protected.

IoT Security Best Practices

To mitigate the risks associated with IoT devices, it is crucial to follow best practices for IoT security. Consider the following measures:

Secure Device Management: Change default usernames and passwords on IoT devices to unique and strong credentials. Regularly update device firmware and apply security patches provided by the manufacturers.

Network Segmentation: Segment your home or office network to isolate IoT devices from critical systems and sensitive data. This helps contain potential breaches and limits the impact of compromised devices.

Implement Strong Network Security: Secure your Wi-Fi network with a strong password and enable encryption, such as WPA2 or WPA3. Disable any unnecessary network services and guest access features to reduce potential attack surfaces.

Monitor and Manage Device Access: Regularly review and manage the access privileges of IoT devices. Remove or disable unnecessary features or services that are not actively used to minimize potential vulnerabilities.

Securing Smart Home Devices

Smart home devices, such as voice assistants, smart thermostats, and security cameras, are increasingly popular. However, they can pose unique security challenges. Consider the following practices to secure your smart home devices:

Change Default Settings: Modify default settings and credentials on smart home devices. Create strong and unique passwords and enable multi-factor authentication whenever possible.

Keep Firmware Up to Date: Regularly update the firmware of smart home devices to ensure they have the latest security patches. Check for updates from the manufacturers' websites or through their respective mobile apps.

Secure your Home Network: Secure your home Wi-Fi network, as discussed in Chapter 9. Implement strong encryption, change default router settings, and disable remote administration features to prevent unauthorized access.

Review Device Permissions: Review and limit the permissions granted to smart home devices. Only grant necessary access to functions and services and be cautious of devices that request excessive permissions or access to sensitive data.

Privacy Concerns with IoT Devices

Privacy is a major concern with IoT devices, as they collect and process vast amounts of personal data. Take the following steps to address privacy concerns:

Read Privacy Policies: Review the privacy policies of IoT devices and services before using them. Understand how your data will be collected, stored, and shared, and ensure the policies align with your privacy preferences.

Disable Unnecessary Data Collection: Disable any data collection or sharing features that are not essential for the device's functionality. Be mindful of the data you share and consider the trade-offs between convenience and privacy.

Secure Data Transmission: Ensure that data transmitted by IoT devices is encrypted and transmitted securely over the internet. Look for devices that use encryption protocols, such as SSL/TLS, to protect data in transit.

Regularly Review Connected Devices: Periodically review the

IoT devices connected to your network, including smart home devices, smart TVs, voice assistants, and other Internet of Things (IoT) devices.

CHAPTER 14: CYBERSECURITY FOR CHILDREN AND FAMILIES

Online Safety for Children

Ensuring the online safety of children is paramount in today's digital age. This chapter focuses on strategies and practices to promote a safe online environment for children:

Open Communication: Establish open and ongoing communication with children about their online activities. Encourage them to share any concerns or incidents they may encounter while using the internet.

Age-Appropriate Content: Educate children about age-appropriate content and help them understand the importance of avoiding inappropriate websites, social media interactions, or online games.

Personal Information Protection: Teach children about the significance of safeguarding personal information online. Instruct them not to share sensitive details, such as full names, addresses, phone numbers, or school information, without parental permission.

Parental Controls and Monitoring

Parental controls and monitoring tools are essential in managing and protecting children's online experiences. Consider the following measures:

Content Filtering: Enable content filtering mechanisms on devices, routers, or web browsers to restrict access to inappropriate or harmful content. Configure filters based on the child's age and specific needs.

Time Restrictions: Set limits on the amount of time children can spend online. Implement time restrictions to prevent excessive screen time and promote a healthy balance between online and offline activities.

Monitoring Software: Utilize monitoring software to track and monitor children's online activities. These tools can provide insights into the websites visited, applications used, and social media interactions, allowing parents to identify potential risks or threats.

Educating Children about
Online Threats

Education is key to empowering children to navigate the online world safely. Teach them about common online threats and best practices:

Cyberbullying Awareness: Educate children about the risks and consequences of cyberbullying. Encourage them to treat others with kindness and empathy, and to report any instances of cyberbullying to a trusted adult.

Phishing and Scams: Teach children to recognize phishing emails, messages, or pop-ups that may try to trick them into sharing personal information or downloading malware. Emphasize the importance of not clicking on suspicious links or opening attachments from unknown sources.

Social Media Safety: Educate children about the potential risks associated with social media platforms, such as privacy settings, sharing personal information, and interacting with strangers. Encourage responsible use of social media and guide them on appropriate online behavior.

Safe Internet Usage Guidelines

Establishing safe internet usage guidelines helps children develop responsible online habits. Consider implementing the following guidelines:

Use Strong and Unique Passwords: Teach children about the importance of creating strong and unique passwords for their online accounts. Emphasize the importance of not sharing passwords with anyone, including friends.

Privacy Settings: Instruct children on how to adjust privacy settings on their social media accounts and other online platforms to limit the visibility of their personal information.

Reporting Concerns: Encourage children to report any concerning or inappropriate content they come across online to a trusted adult, such as a parent, teacher, or school counselor. Establish a supportive environment where children feel comfortable seeking help or advice.

Safe Online Behavior: Teach children about responsible online behavior, including treating others with respect, refraining from sharing inappropriate content, and not engaging in online arguments or conflicts.

By implementing parental controls, engaging in open communication, educating children about online threats, and setting safe internet usage guidelines, parents can create a secure online environment for their children and promote responsible digital citizenship.

CHAPTER 15: EMERGING CYBERSECURITY TRENDS AND TECHNOLOGIES

Artificial Intelligence and Machine Learning in Cybersecurity

A rtificial Intelligence (AI) and Machine Learning (ML) have emerged as powerful tools in the field of cybersecurity. This chapter explores their applications and benefits:

Threat Detection and Prevention: AI and ML algorithms can analyze large volumes of data to detect patterns and anomalies that indicate potential cyber threats. They can help identify malware, phishing attempts, and other malicious activities in real-time, enhancing the ability to prevent and respond to attacks.

Behavioral Analysis: AI and ML can analyze user behavior to establish baselines and identify deviations that may indicate unauthorized access or suspicious activity. This enables proactive threat detection and enhances security measures.

Automated Response and Remediation: AI and ML can automate the response to security incidents, enabling faster and more effective incident handling. They can autonomously identify and neutralize threats, reducing response time and minimizing the impact of attacks.

Blockchain and Cybersecurity

Blockchain technology has gained significant attention not only in the realm of cryptocurrencies but also in the field of cybersecurity. This section explores the potential applications of blockchain for enhancing security:

Immutable and Transparent Recordkeeping: The decentralized nature of blockchain provides tamper-proof and transparent recordkeeping. This can enhance data integrity, authentication, and verification processes, reducing the risk of data manipulation or unauthorized access.

Secure Transactions: Blockchain technology can facilitate secure transactions by eliminating the need for intermediaries and providing robust cryptographic mechanisms. This can enhance the security of financial transactions, supply chain management, and identity verification processes.

Decentralized Identity Management: Blockchain can enable decentralized and self-sovereign identity management, where individuals have control over their personal data. This reduces reliance on centralized databases, mitigates the risk of data breaches, and enhances privacy.

Cloud Security Considerations

As more organizations adopt cloud computing services, understanding cloud security considerations becomes crucial. This section highlights key aspects of cloud security:

Data Encryption: Ensure that data stored in the cloud is encrypted both at rest and in transit. Encryption provides an additional layer of protection, safeguarding sensitive information from unauthorized access.

Access Management: Implement strong access controls and

authentication mechanisms to restrict access to cloud resources. Use multi-factor authentication and regularly review access privileges to prevent unauthorized access.

Secure Configuration: Follow best practices for configuring cloud services and ensure that default security settings are modified to meet your organization's specific security requirements. Regularly assess and update security configurations as needed.

Data Backup and Recovery: Establish robust backup and recovery processes for data stored in the cloud. Regularly back up critical data to prevent data loss in the event of a security incident or system failure.

Biometric Security and Authentication

Biometric security and authentication methods, such as fingerprint scanning, facial recognition, and iris scanning, offer enhanced security and user convenience. This section explores the applications and considerations of biometric security:

Unique Identification: Biometric authentication relies on unique biological characteristics to identify individuals, making it difficult for attackers to replicate or forge credentials.

User Convenience: Biometric authentication methods offer a seamless and user-friendly experience, eliminating the need to remember complex passwords or PINs.

Considerations and Privacy: While biometric authentication provides enhanced security, it also raises privacy concerns. Organizations must manage biometric data ethically, ensuring appropriate storage, usage, and protection in compliance with relevant privacy regulations.

Multifactor Authentication: Biometric authentication is often used as part of a multifactor authentication approach, combining biometrics with other factors such as passwords or tokens for enhanced security.

By staying updated on emerging cybersecurity trends and technologies, organizations can proactively adapt their security strategies and leverage these advancements to strengthen their defense against evolving cyber threats.

CHAPTER 16: CONCLUSION

Recap of Key Takeaways

Throughout this book, we have covered a wide range of topics related to cybersecurity. Let us recap some of the key takeaways:

◆ ◆ ◆

- Cybersecurity is essential in today's digital landscape to protect individuals, organizations, and critical infrastructure from cyber threats.

◆ ◆ ◆

- Cybercriminals employ various tactics, such as phishing, malware, ransomware, and social engineering, to exploit vulnerabilities and gain unauthorized access to systems and data.

◆ ◆ ◆

- Password security is crucial. Use strong and unique passwords, enable two-factor authentication, and regularly update passwords to protect against unauthorized access.

◆ ◆ ◆

- Phishing emails are common. Recognize the signs of phishing emails, such as suspicious senders, grammatical errors, and urgent requests for personal information, and avoid clicking on suspicious links or downloading attachments.

◆ ◆ ◆

- Secure your mobile devices by enabling device passcodes, using biometric authentication, keeping software and apps up to date, and installing reputable security software.

- Safeguard your home network by securing your Wi-Fi network, implementing router security best practices, using network firewalls and intrusion detection systems, and regularly updating software.

- Backup your important data regularly and consider using cloud backup solutions or external storage devices to ensure data recovery in case of data loss or system failure.

- Practice safe online shopping and banking by using secure websites, avoiding public Wi-Fi for financial transactions, and regularly monitoring your financial accounts for any suspicious activity.

- Employee cybersecurity training is essential to create a security-conscious workplace culture. Regular training and updates can help employees recognize and respond to security incidents effectively.

- As the Internet of Things (IoT) grows, secure your IoT devices by changing default passwords, updating firmware, and isolating IoT devices from your main network to minimize potential risks.

- Protect children and promote online safety by establishing open communication, using parental controls and monitoring tools, educating children about online threats, and setting safe internet usage guidelines.

- Stay informed about emerging cybersecurity trends and technologies, such as artificial intelligence, blockchain, cloud security, and biometric authentication, to enhance your cybersecurity defenses.

Final Thoughts on Cybersecurity

Cybersecurity is a dynamic field that requires continuous learning, adaptation, and vigilance. It is crucial for individuals, businesses, and society to prioritize cybersecurity to mitigate risks and protect sensitive information.

By implementing the best practices outlined in this book, staying informed about the latest threats and technologies, and fostering a culture of security awareness, you can significantly reduce the likelihood of falling victim to cyber-attacks.

Remember that cybersecurity is a shared responsibility. It is essential to collaborate with organizations, governments, and technology providers to collectively strengthen the overall security posture and promote a safer digital ecosystem for everyone.

Stay proactive, stay informed, and stay secure. Together, we can create a more resilient and secure digital world.

CYBERSECURITY RESOURCES

Organizations and Links for Reference and Training

Cybersecurity Organizations And Websites:

- National Institute of Standards and Technology (NIST): https://www.nist.gov/cybersecurity

- Cybersecurity and Infrastructure Security Agency (CISA): https://www.cisa.gov/cybersecurity

Online Courses And Training Platforms:

- Coursera: https://www.coursera.org/

- Udemy: https://www.udemy.com/

- Cybrary: https://www.cybrary.it/

- SANS Institute: https://www.sans.org/ cyber-security-courses/

Security Blogs And News Sources:

- Krebs on Security: https://krebsonsecurity.com/

- The Hacker News: https://thehackernews.com/

- Dark Reading: https://www.darkreading.com/

- Threatpost: https://threatpost.com/

Security Standards And Best Practices:

- NIST Cybersecurity Framework: https://www.nist.gov/cyberframework

Please note that the inclusion of specific resources and tools does not imply endorsement or guarantee of their effectiveness. It is always recommended to conduct your own research and evaluation before using any tools or services.

Password Keepers And Generators

LastPass: LastPass is a popular password manager that securely stores and generates passwords. It offers browser extensions, mobile apps, and cloud syncing capabilities. Website: https://www.lastpass.com/

Dashlane: Dashlane is another widely used password manager that offers password generation, autofill, and secure storage. It supports multiple platforms and provides additional features like password sharing and a digital wallet. Website: https://www.dashlane.com/

KeePass: KeePass is an open-source password manager that allows you to generate, store, and manage passwords locally. It provides strong encryption and can be used on various platforms. Website: https://keepass.info/

1Password: 1Password is a password manager that offers features like password generation, autofill, and secure storage. It supports multiple devices and platforms, including desktop and mobile. Website: https://1password.com/

Bitwarden: Bitwarden is a free and open-source password manager that provides secure password storage and generation. It offers browser extensions, mobile apps, and self-hosted options. Website: https://bitwarden.com/

Random.org: Random.org is a website that offers a random number generator, which can be used to generate random passwords. It allows you to specify the length and complexity of the password. Website: https://www.random.org/passwords/

Norton Password Generator: Norton Password Generator is an online tool provided by Norton, which generates random and secure passwords. It allows you to choose the length and complexity of the password. Website: https://passwords.norton.com/

Remember to choose a reputable password manager or generator and follow best practices for using them, such as using a strong primary password, enabling two-factor authentication, and regularly updating your passwords.

Resources On Cyberbullying And Online Safety For Kids

National Online Safety: National Online Safety provides resources, guides, and courses to educate parents, teachers, and children about online safety, including topics like cyberbullying. Website: https://nationalonlinesafety.com/

Common Sense Media: Common Sense Media offers a range of resources, tips, and advice for parents on how to keep their kids safe online. They provide reviews of apps, games, and websites to help parents make informed decisions. Website: https://www.commonsensemedia.org/

Net Nanny: Net Nanny is a parental control software that allows you to monitor and filter your child's online activities, block inappropriate content, and set time limits. It provides real-time alerts and reporting features. Website: https://www.netnanny.com/

Bark: Bark is a monitoring service that uses artificial intelligence to detect potential dangers and risks in your child's online activities, including cyberbullying, online predators, and inappropriate content. Website: https://www.bark.us/

Mobicip: Mobicip is parental control software that enables you to manage and monitor your child's internet usage across multiple devices. It offers content filtering, time restrictions, and activity reports. Website: https://www.mobicip.com/

Google Family Link: Google Family Link is a parental control app that allows you to set digital ground rules for your child's device usage. It provides features like screen time limits, app monitoring, and content filters. Website: https://families.google.com/familylink/

The Cyberbullying Research Center: The Cyberbullying Research Center provides resources, research, and advice on preventing and addressing cyberbullying. They offer tips for parents, educators, and students. Website: https://cyberbullying.org/

StopBullying.gov: StopBullying.gov is a U.S. government website that provides information and resources on preventing and responding to bullying, including cyberbullying. It offers guidance for parents, educators, and kids. Website: https://www.stopbullying.gov/

Remember, it is important to have open and ongoing conversations with your children about online safety, encourage them to report any cyberbullying incidents, and teach them how to be responsible using digital platforms.

Employee Cybersecurity Training:

SANS Securing the Human: SANS Securing the Human offers

a variety of cybersecurity training programs and resources specifically designed for employees. They provide interactive training modules, videos, newsletters, and posters to raise awareness and educate employees about cybersecurity best practices. Website: https://www.sans.org/security-awareness-training

KnowBe4: KnowBe4 is a popular security awareness training platform that offers a wide range of interactive training modules, simulated phishing campaigns, and security awareness resources. They provide customizable training programs to suit different organizational needs. Website: https://www.knowbe4.com/

PhishMe: PhishMe, now part of Cofense, provides phishing simulation and training solutions. They offer interactive training modules, phishing email templates, and reporting tools to help organizations train employees to recognize and respond to phishing attacks. Website: https://cofense.com/

InfoSec Institute: InfoSec Institute offers cybersecurity training courses, including employee awareness training. They cover topics such as social engineering, phishing, password security, and secure email practices. Website: https://www.infosecinstitute.com/

Security Mentor: Security Mentor provides a comprehensive library of online security awareness training courses. They offer engaging, interactive modules on various cybersecurity topics, including secure computing, mobile device security, and safe web browsing. Website: https://www.securitymentor.com/

National Cyber Security Centre (NCSC): The NCSC offers free cybersecurity training resources and guidance for businesses and employees. They provide e-learning modules, toolkits, and best practice guides to help organizations improve their security awareness. Website: https://www.ncsc.gov.uk/collection/training-resources

Cybrary: Cybrary is an online platform that offers a wide range of cybersecurity training courses, including courses suitable for employee training. They cover topics such as cybersecurity awareness, secure coding, and incident response. Website: https://www.cybrary.it/

Udemy: Udemy is an online learning platform that offers a variety of cybersecurity courses. They have courses designed for employees, covering topics like cybersecurity awareness, data protection, and secure communication. Website: https://www.udemy.com/

Remember, effective cybersecurity training should be an ongoing process. It is important to regularly reinforce and update training materials to keep up with emerging threats and evolving best practices. Additionally, consider customizing training programs to align with your organization's specific needs and risk profile.

ACKNOWLEDGEMENT

All Images From Pixabay - Image Creators Listed Below

Cliff Hang

◆ ◆ ◆

Thomas Breher

◆ ◆ ◆

Jonathan Hammond

◆ ◆ ◆

Gerd Altmann

ABOUT THE AUTHOR

D. L. Freeman

D. L. Freeman has spent more than twenty years of his career in the technology industry. He has worked for critical infrastructure organizations with a role of ensuring Reliability, Business Continuity, and Data Security.

He has directed and implemented Cybersecurity measures and best practices including, the education and training of employees.

He has had the privilege to work alongside multiple organizations and professionals in collaboration with the end goal of Cybersecurity Implementation and Awareness.

Made in the USA
Las Vegas, NV
26 November 2023

81579511R00046